Phyllis Chockouski

Legacy
of
Love

Legacy of Love

Poems by Joanne Ginsberg

Photographs by Ruth Orkin

GROSSET & DUNLAP, INC.

A NATIONAL GENERAL COMPANY

Publishers • New York

Library of Congress Catalog Card No: 72-158758
ISBN: 0-448-00643-X

Printed in the United States of America

Carl Sandburg called one of his collections
"The People Yes." Joanne Ginsberg's poems could be called
"The Person Yes." It is not that Mrs. Ginsberg is unconcerned
with humanity at large—the oppressions and frustrations
of urban life, the obscenity of war—
but the best (and the most) of her poems are
about the individual trying to make sense, or make a
viable adjustment to the nonsense, of Life itself.
And this theme ranges in treatment from the lyricism
of love poems to the compact quatrains that make
philosophical statements (or ask philosophical questions),
and including a few single sentences setting down
something that she has noticed (and that we notice
after reading her)—for instance, that
"the friendliest people at airports are babies."

MAURICE DOLBIER

Gerry:
I waded 'cross the stream
    removing
        weeds and rocks
Releasing
    my soul
. . . to reach you

Legacy of Love

It's raining today
    and my eyes are full of you
My mind leaves the clouded skies
    and rests
        on a pillow of May sunshine
May
    a month of dreams
        my month of hope
My heart had been nourished
    as the earth below my fingertips
        had drunk from the springs
            of winter's snows

I clung to the mastery of you

It's raining today
    and my ears are listening
        and now I know
That forever
    is today
        and every tomorrow
            that will be yesterday

It's raining today
    and my mouth forms words
. . . be gentle with her

The rain will stop
   and clouds will fade away
But she could feed the plants of life
   today
     tomorrow
. . . and yesterday □

Being
   a woman
Is like
   being
      a person

It isn't something
   you
      turn-on or turn-off
You simply
   are

If
   you are □

When I was younger
   I didn't know
      what
         I didn't know

I could cry
   if
      things didn't go my way

I wasn't responsible
   for
      what I said

Because
   I still
      had rocks in my head

I was free to explore
    what
        I couldn't ignore

I could
    accept or reject
        as I saw fit

And if I was confused
    I could
        stamp on the floor

I was never confined
    to the rules that make
        grown-ups blind

Now I'm older . . . □

All
    the brilliant
        conversations
All
    the instant
        observations
All
    at once
        a new sensation
Then
    the shocking
        revelation
You
    might well be
. . . in love with me □

I'm so sloppy
    I never think
        to put things back
            or hang up clothes
My mind
    is always cluttered
    . . . with you □

A kiss can say
. . . don't go away

Come
   lie next to me
We'll watch the sun slip away
   giving birth to another day
      on the other side
. . . of God's face □

    I need you so much tonight—to touch
the words like blind hands across a page of
braille . . .
    I need you to kiss my failures—and
not decry that they exist but love me more
for each one . . .
    I need your tears to give me strength . . .
    I need to bite into your shoulder with
an angry mind that wants to lick its wounds . . .
    To smell the maleness of sweat that pours
like oily perfume from your scalp and makes
me know that I am woman . . .
    I need to scream at me by teasing you—
until you do . . .
    I need your force to let me know I give
you power to overpower me . . .
    I need you so tonight . . . □

24

What do you think
　　when you drink your morning coffee?

At mid-day
　　when we're apart
　　　　What do you say to yourself?

Do you really like me
　　or do I breed
　　　　just a need in you?

Will you still love me
　　when the folds appear
　　　　upon this smooth veneer?

Were I to hand you me
　　open-up the cavity
. . . could you survive the flood? □

God's chemistry:

The fusion of two souls adrift
. . . melding into one □

Your mouth and ears
      were mine
For giving
      tasting
For listening . . .
      burned
           concerned

Your hands have cradled mine
      through grief-torn
           joy-born times

Your eyes sought mine
      a hundred times
           deliberate
                determined
. . . I love you □

If I could love you less
     you could need me more
I could mark the battlefield
     saving you the scars
          of life-long war

If I could love you less
     you could need me more
You could speak to me of conflicts
     plow your depths of fear
You could bear the pain of saying
     "Stay away, my dear
          but for this moment
               take my hand
. . . I do not need you near"□

I wait
  beneath you
    in the valley
      pregnant with pain

Soon
  you'll rise
    and be gone
. . . my king □

Why do I enrage you so
   because I say I know
      what's right for me

Why do you always look
   for the flaws
      in what I say
My feet
   like yours
      are made of clay

If you must
   shoot me down
      to survive the life
         of this clown-town
I'd best leave you now
   before I drown
   . . . in a sea of pity □

When confusion wrapped my mind in endless thought
     and fear began to penetrate my being
For I knew not
     who I was
          nor where to go
You smiled, and said
     you're growing

When the mystery of love
     dissolved the selfish world
          in which I lived
               and cast me out forever
Discharging every garment of protection
     pride
          and ego
               from my service
You smiled, and said
     you're growing

When the joy of giving
    became my only source of strength
        and my shadow
            my bedmate
You smiled, and said
    you've grown
You have earned the right
. . . to live alone □

The answer was that we simply couldn't live together, Your Honor. Why must the facts be black or white? Why must you find valid grounds in order to substantiate the fact that two sad souls can no longer sleep together? There is no right or wrong in this divorce case, only great pain for what remains—nothing . . .

There is no dignity in seeing a man—the man—who planted the seeds of life in your body—cry . . . □

My darling children,
    there are no shattered mirrors
        but those that fall
            because they must

There are no broken windows
    but those that break
        because the frame is weak

There are no broken hearts, my loves
    but those that break
. . . because they fail to beat □

Night Words:

The screaming silence
     of the dark
My bed so cold
     my love and I
. . . apart □

My window
  closed
    against the cold
I watched the snow
  as it rolled
    across the window-pane
. . . and down my cheek □

How long can you live
  with a moment

A lifetime
. . . or maybe longer □

Do you know
    the friendliest people
        at airports
            are babies □

If only
I had sealed your words
inside a wax-tight
sterile bottle
. . . for use today □

Alone's
　　not sharing morning coffee
　　　　nor turning in my sleep
　　　　　　to meet your mouth
　　　　　　　　and find your hand beneath the sheet
. . . secure

Alone's
　　not crying in my sleep
. . . it's sleeping alone □

Today
    I must breathe
      the words
        into my soul

LIVIN'
   is
     GIVIN'
and you
. . . you're a midwife of life □

Let me
   hold life
      close to my breast
. . . like an empty treasure chest

Let me
   fill it
      with love

Let me
   "will it"
      to my children □

51

Maybe tomorrow
    I'll swallow the fact
I had no one to run with
    today

Maybe in time
    I'll learn to climb
The rocks by the seashore
    alone

Maybe the years
    will grant me grace
       to forget his face
Yet leave a trace
. . . of my love □

Save me
   soft night
      from melancholy

Paint me a picture of brilliant colors

Take me
   soft night
      and let me wander
         near the sea
Up and down fog-banked lanes
   where no car can travel
Make me a coat of mist and dew
   to shroud my body
      with a lover's warmth

Walk with me
   soft night
      thru the painted picture
. . . and beyond □

Open up
and
. . . outcomes you □

Gently
    you came into my life
You saw
    the tenseness and fear
        beneath the smooth veneer

Gently
    you took my hand
        and understood the sand
            on which I walked
                was not the earth
                    to which I clung

Gently
    you opened up
        the blind mind
            to hope

Somewhere
    you saw
        the gnawing pain
My fear
. . . to draw you near □

Hey
   come play
      in my garden
Pardon
   my sin
      of self-concern
Forgive me
   I didn't see
      your sadness

We are one
   you and I
      don't shy away
Come share
   a
      play-day
         with me
I'll let you
   win
      if you'll please
         come in
Hey
   come play
. . . in my garden □

I didn't believe
that a someone like you
. . . existed

I'd looked into mirrors
so many times
and found bound souls
. . . blind minds

I don't know if I
can defy the years
But when we're together
. . . I can allay the fears □

The sky
    is my beach
The clouds
    a lap
        to rest
            an airborne mind

I cannot see
    the birds below
Yet
    I can hear
        their singing

. . . stay away, closer □

Although
    I cannot watch you
        as your mouth pursues the words
            that make the emptiness of separation disappear
  I can trace the rim of mine
    and find your smile

Although
    I cannot touch the tears
        that echo in the quiet of your voice
  I must walk thru the mist
    that frames my eyes
        to you

For I am your tomorrow
    and you my love
  . . . are mine □

I pray my words
. . . will speak for me

Goodnight Roberta
Goodnight Sasha